STOP LIVING PAYCHECK TO PAYCHECK

AF127584

BOB ALLEN

FALL ON YOUR CHIN

FRANNY SYUFY

GO AU NATURAL

TOBY GRAY

ROB BUY

MR.PT.LEE

BINTA ANNAN

DÊSIGNÊR HÂNDBÂGS KNÔCKÔFFS

RÖLËX RËPLICÄS WÄTCHËS

"hello unob—trusive."

Lee Finn

"Space shuttle banana."

Sam Sophomore

"I want to buy your house."

Lee Finn

Shakes her head

Sam Sophomore

"Online sales are boom—ing."

Lee Finn

"T on tu—multuous."

Sam Sophomore

"I'm Woried."

Lee Finn

NO FIRM PLANS HAVE BEEN MADE, AND SINCE THEN SOME ADDITION ELEMENTS HAVE MATERIALIZED THAT I'M NOT AT LIBERTY TO DISCUSS ON THE RECORD AT THIS MOMENT.

FLO K. HUTCHINS

AT THE SAME TIME, THE GAP BETWEEN RICH AND POOR WITHIN COUNTRIES LIKE THE PHILIPPINES CONTINUES TO WIDEN.

ACEVEDO

DON'T BE LEFT OUT, JOIN MILLIONS OF MEN IN THE REVOLUTION.

IAN REED

You might learn some important lessons during those tough times - like Thomas Edison did.

Clayton James

I WASN'T ABLE TO ATTEND, AND IT WOULD BE NICE TO AT LEAST BE ABLE TO READ THE TRANSCRIPT.

TRUJILLO

IT'S OK.

SHERA HIEDI

PAMELA

ARMSTR⊠NG

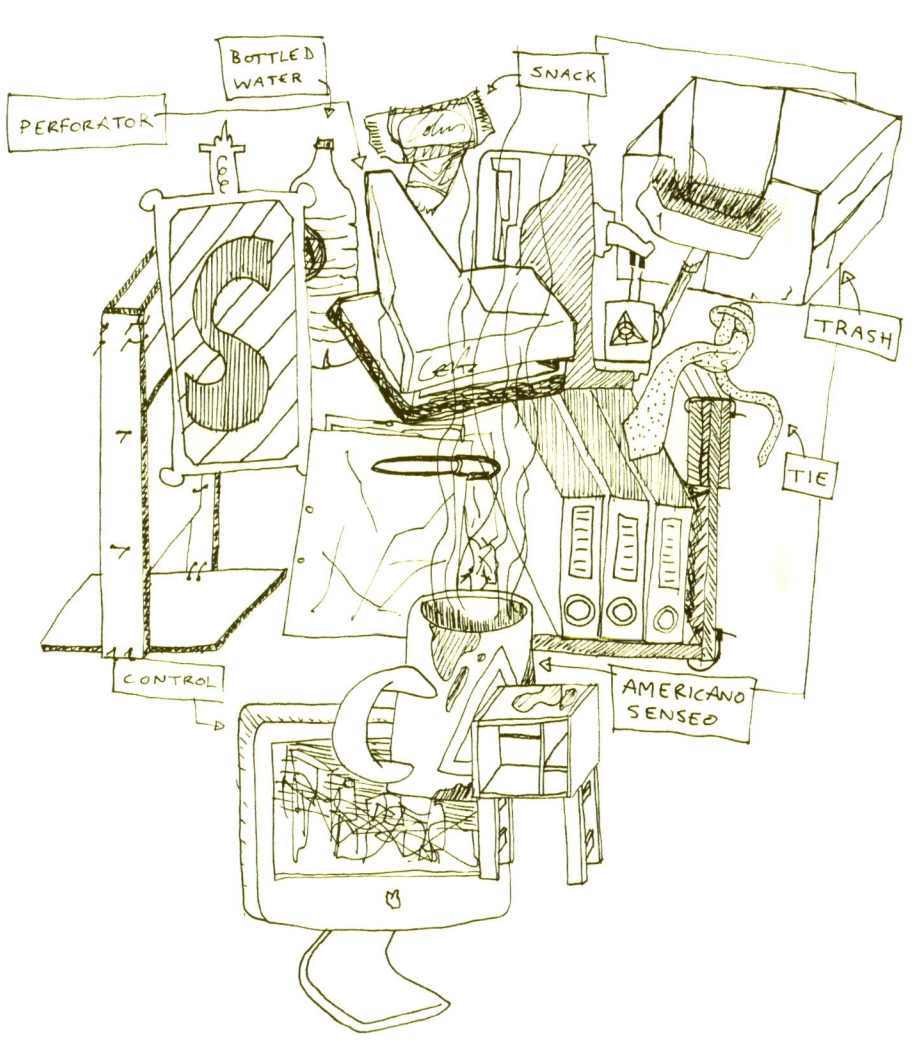

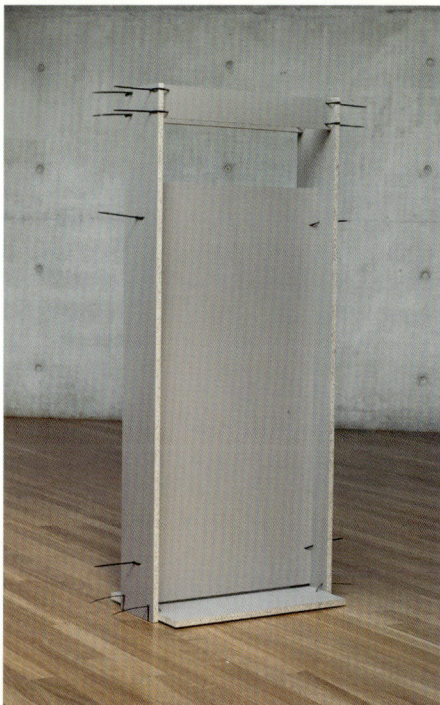

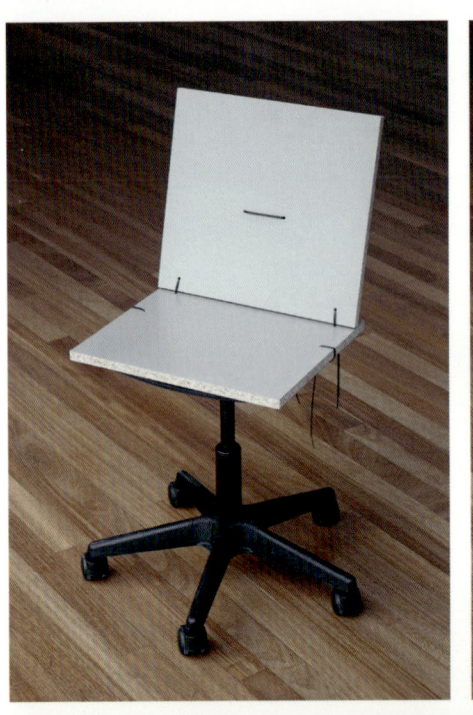

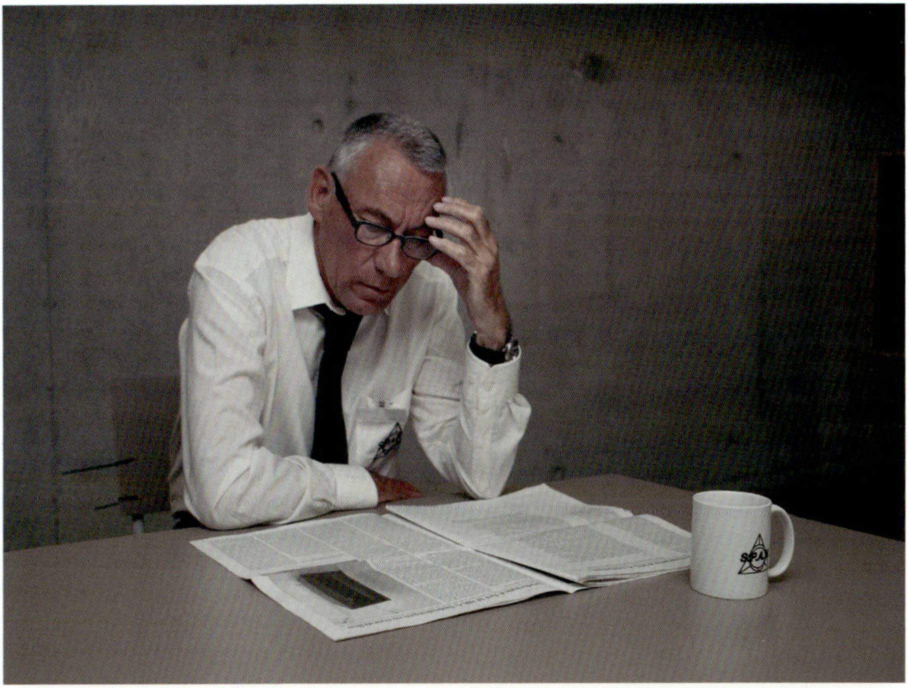

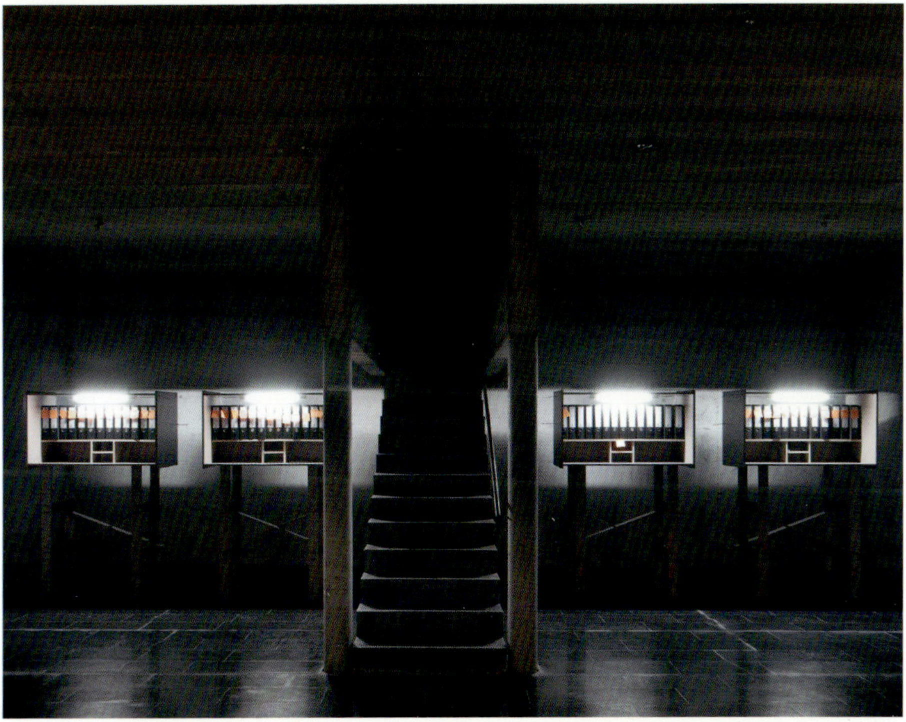

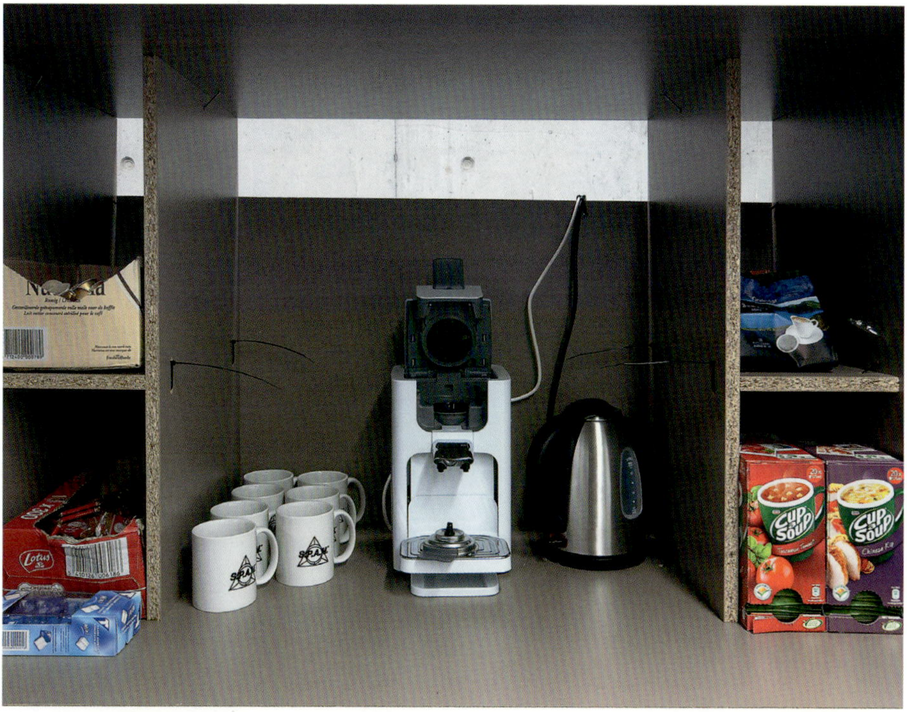

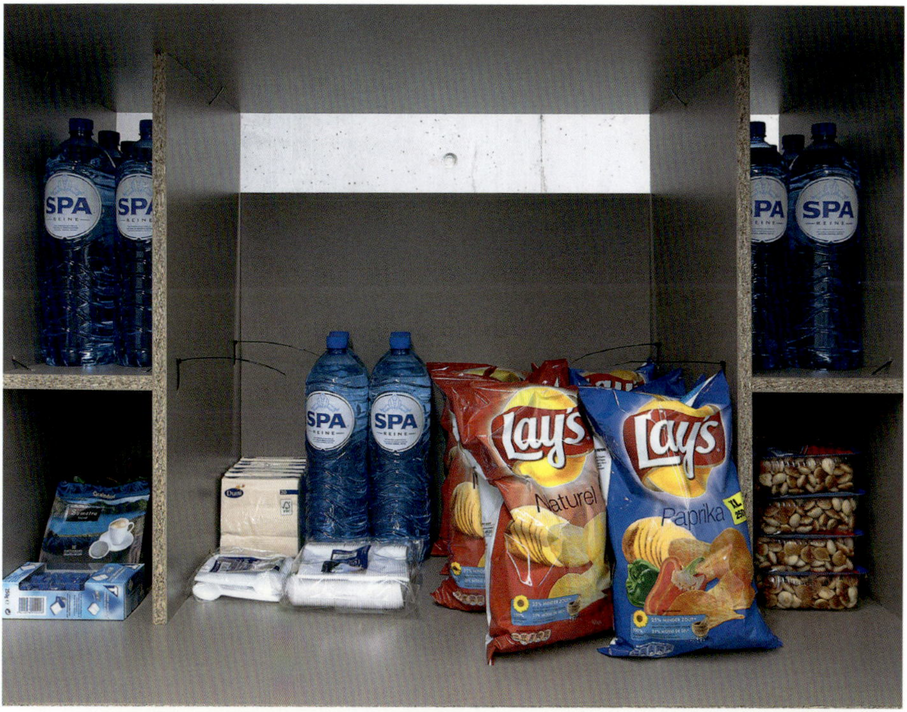
SPA
SPA
SPA
SPA
SPA
SPA
Lay's
Naturel
Lay's
Paprika

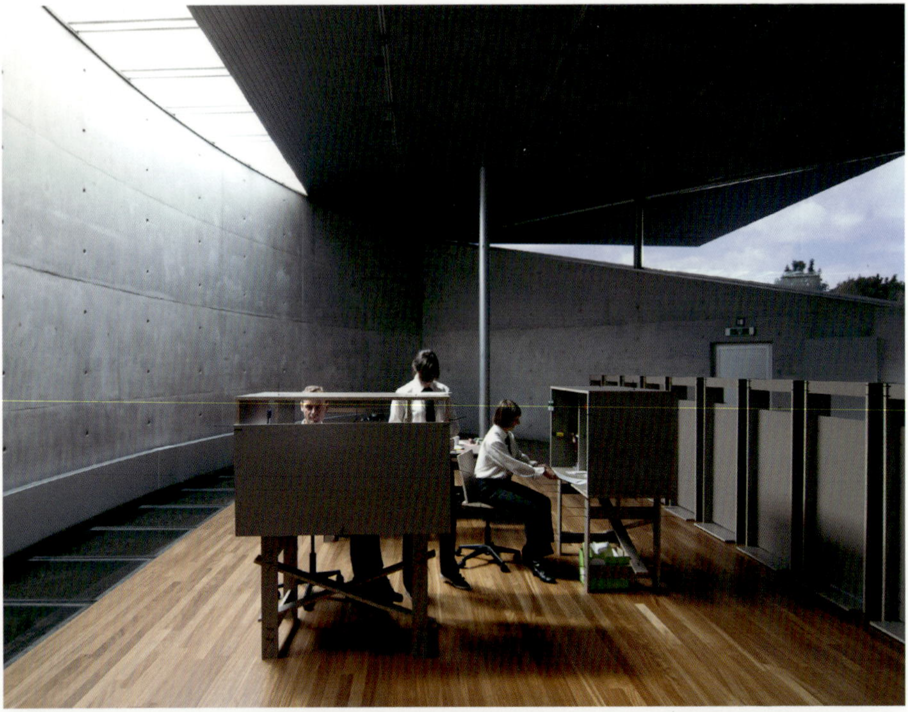

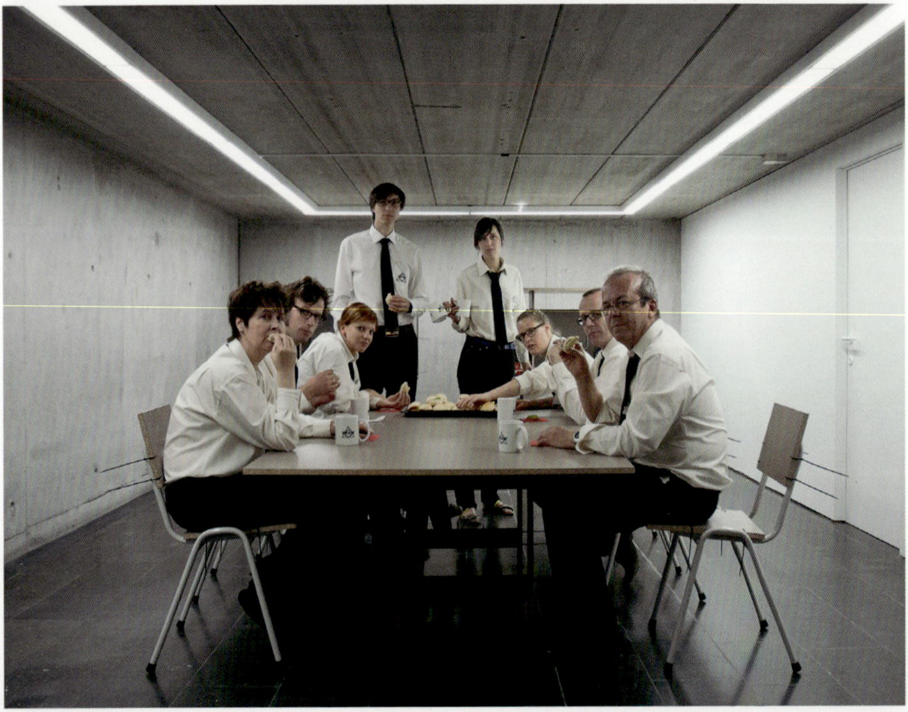

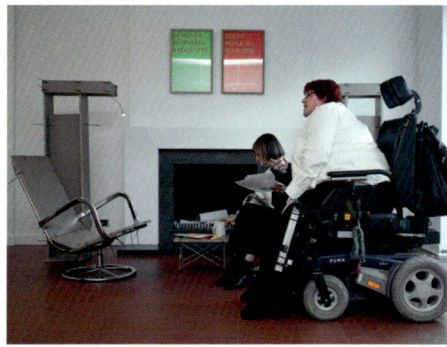

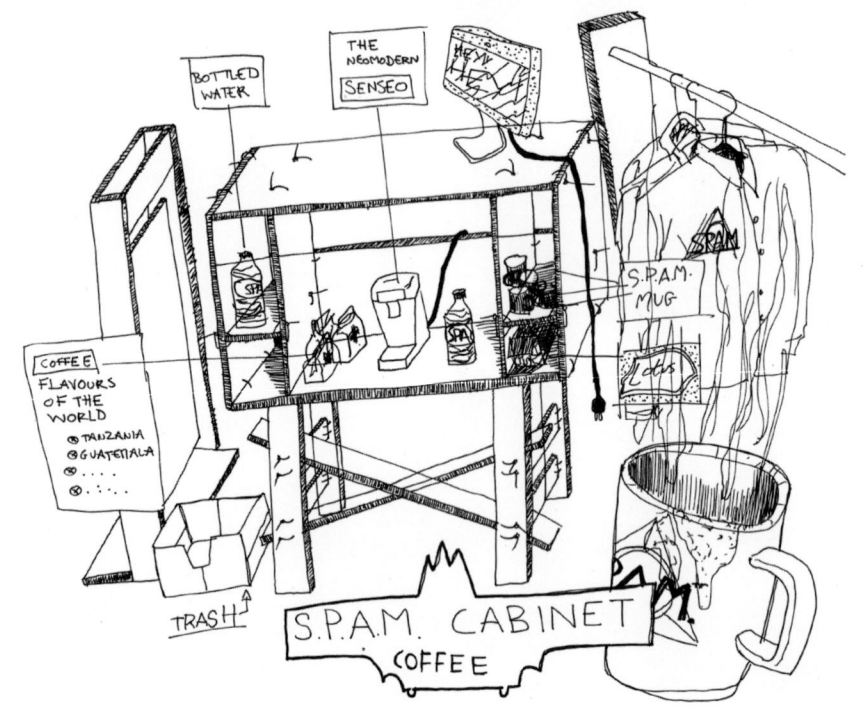

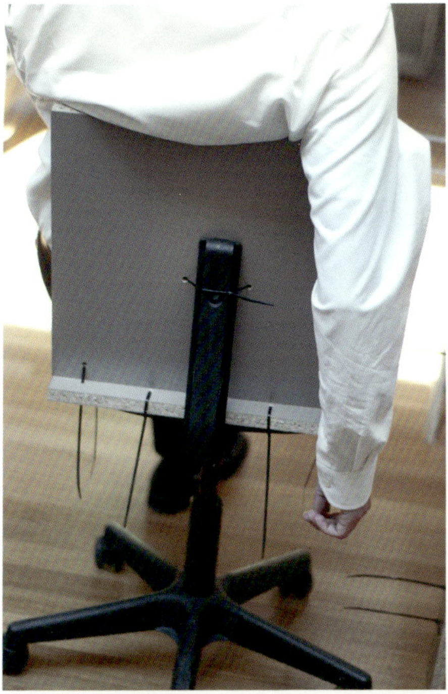

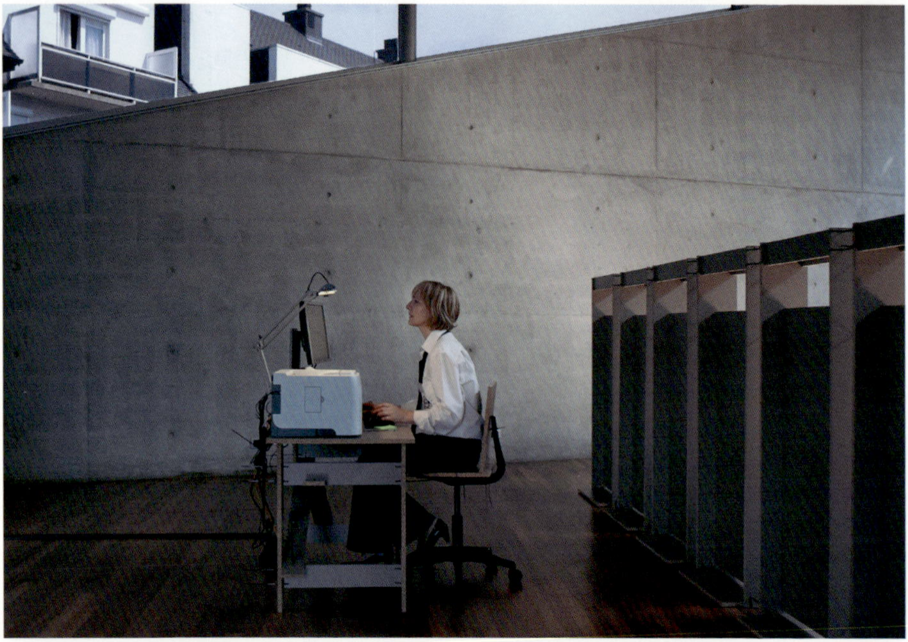

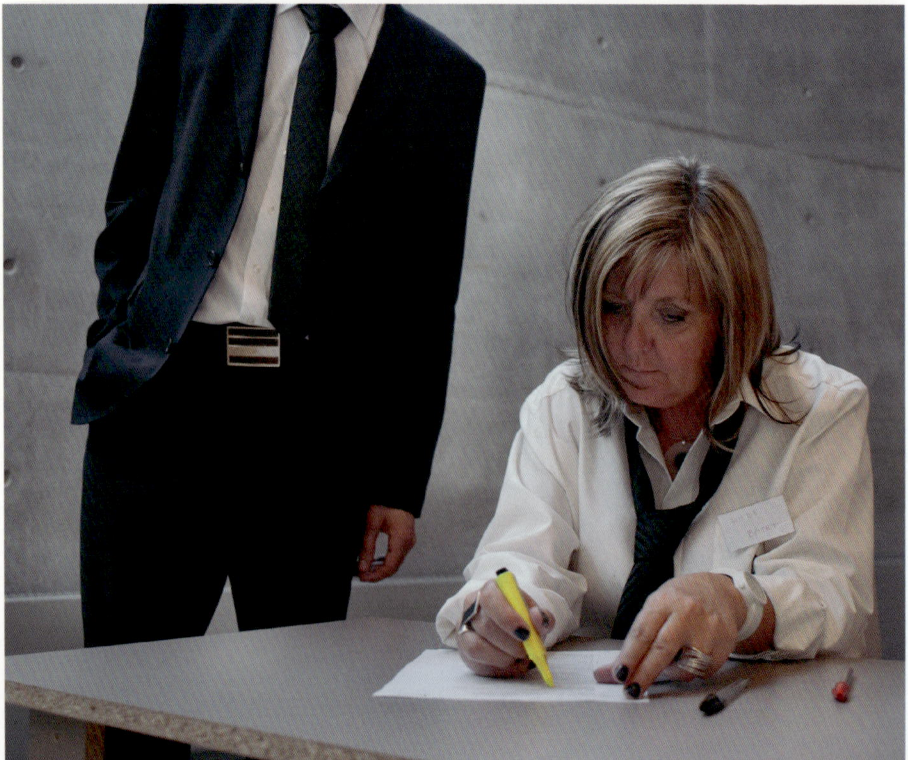

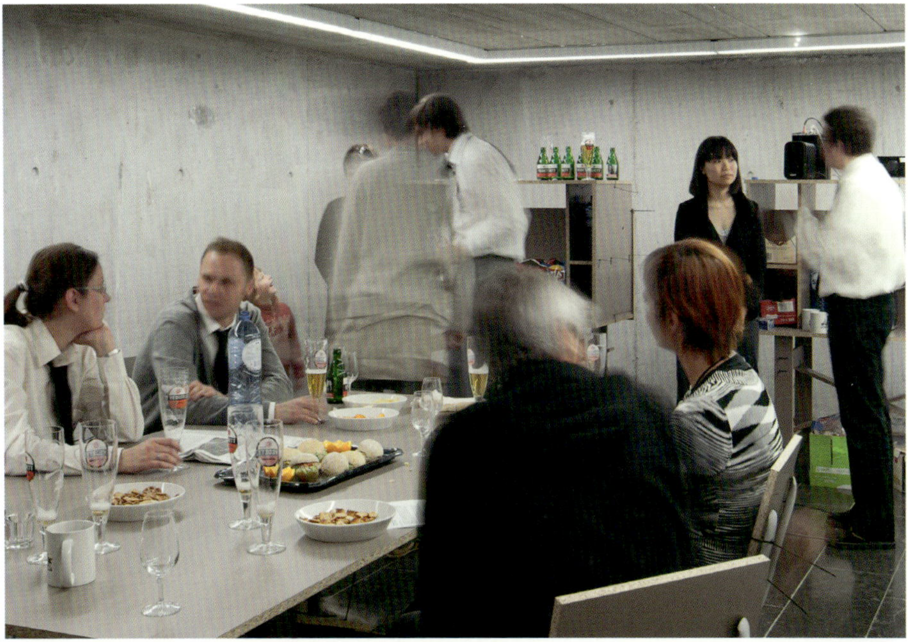

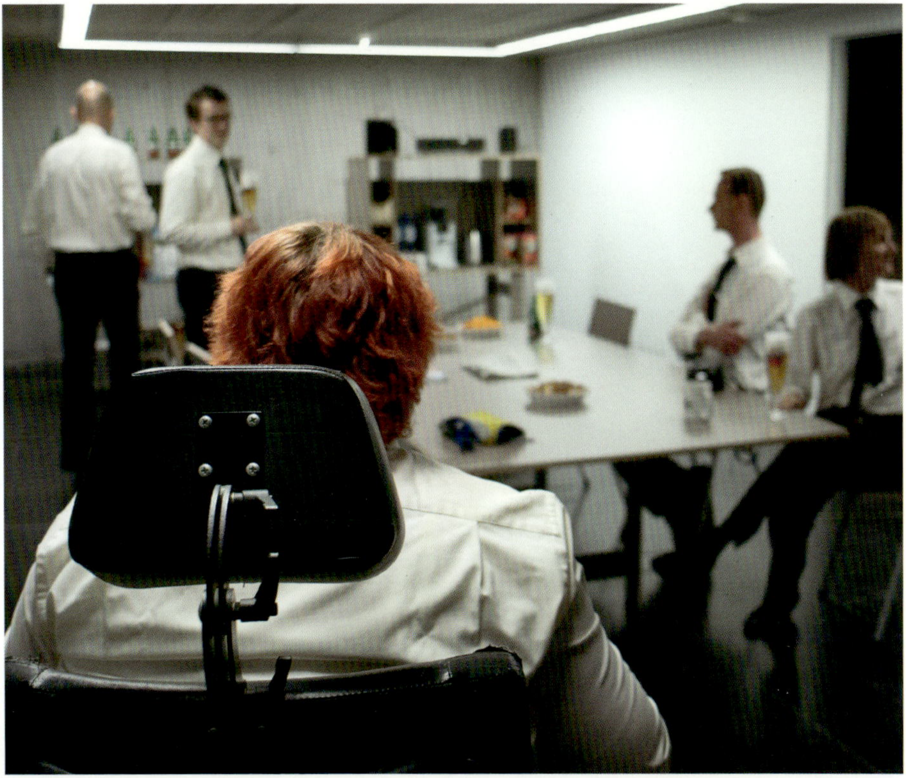

New Rules (1-5), 2010-2011
Photographic print, 120cm x 80cm

Warez n Warez, 2010
Photographic print, 2 x 60cm x 40cm

Lee vs Sam, 2008
Photographic print, 7 x 30cm x 20cm

A World Situation, 2007
Photographic print, 6 x 30cm x 20cm

Pamela, 2011

S.P.A.M. OFFICE, 2010-2011
Installation + Performance

S.P.A.M. MUG, 2010
Unlimited edition, coffee mug

TERRIBLE VACATION.......Tim Toubac

From: **hello@pieterjanginckels.be**
Sent: Thu 4/14/11 10:26 AM
To: s-p-a-m@live.com
    1 attachment
    untitled-[2] (0.8 KB)

I'm sorry for this odd request because it might get to you too urgent but it's because of the situation of things right now, I'm stuck in Cardiff Wales, United Kingdom right now. I came down here on vacation, i was robbed, worse of it is that bags, cash, cards and my cell phone was stolen at GUN POINT, it's such a crazy experience for me, i need help in sorting out the hotel bills, the authorities are not being 100% supportive but the good thing is i still have my passport but don't have enough money to pay the hotel bills and get back home, please i need you to loan me some money, i will refund you as soon as I'm back home, i promise.

Thanks For Helping Me

--
Tim Toubac

Mixing Lube with IcyHot for a prank

From: **SexForums** (notifications@sforumsmail.com)
Sent: Sat 5/07/11 11:55 AM
To: s-p-a-m@live.com

SATURDAY 7TH MAY 2011

Featured Gallery
Check out the 3,479 new pics that were added this week, including:

Our Hottest Members

Hottest Girl:
natalie8=D

Hottest Guy:
thicktrick

Top Members of the month:

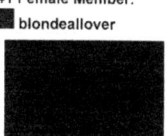

#1 Female Member:
blondeallover

#1 Male Member:
lonely_guy

Featured Stories

Members added 17.528 new stories and comments this week, including:

- The Love Path
- When is a Man so Physically Hot, Women CAN'T Resist?
- Pictures of me (Blondeallover)
- Mixing Lube with IcyHot for a Prank
- Random S3x with Loverboy
- How to make a woman SQUIRT!!!
- Our Story - "Coug" and "Lion" Our Few Days Apart
- Polyfidelity. What do you think?
- Dare to compare (Do you like me shaven or not shaven there?)
- Do you look your age?
- What is your Oral Technique?
- Fast food nation
- Truth or Dare . . .
- A unique way to bind some body parts
- Photos of my wife
- Mental Illness

Top Blogger of the month:

Purrring_Cougar

Say Hi to some of the 3,122 new members this week - Including all the ones from Brussels

geile Steroid University Course 1

From: **isteroids-home@aweber.com** on behalf of **IS Manager** (isteroids.com.manager@gmail.com)
Sent: Sun 12/05/10 12:11 PM
To: geile (s-p-a-m@live.com)

1 attachment
iSteroids-Course1.pdf (45.6 KB)

Hi geile,

We at iSteroids.com are proud to present you the 1st Steroid University learning course out of 10. Please see the Adobe PDF attachment in this email. If you have questions, feel free to ask them on our active forums:
http://forums.isteroids.com

Thanks for your support,
IS Manager

P.O. Box 186, Road Town, Tortola, BVI

To unsubscribe or change subscriber options visit:
http://www.aweber.com/z/r/?rOwMLJystCwcLOys7MzstGa0jKysrEycHA==

STEROID UNIVERSITY

Course syllabus

Course 1 – What are anabolic steroids

Course 2 - How do anabolic Steroids Work

Course 3 – The History of Anabolic Steroids

Course 4 - The benefits of Steroid Use

Course 5 – The Negative Effects of Steroid Use

Course 6 – Oral Vs. Injectable steroids

Course 7 - how to do an injection

Course 8 – Where to administer an injection

Course 9 - How to design an aas cycle

Course 10- Sample Cycles

(No Subject)

From: **Pieterjan Ginckels** (hello@pieterjanginckels.be)
Sent: Wed 2/23/11 8:12 PM
To: s-p-a-m@live.com

> From: **Pamela Armstrong** <pamela180574@hotmail.com>
> Date: Sat 27 Mar 2010 11:34:49 CEST
> To: <hello@pieterjanginckels.be>
>
> Dear friend,
> we are an international electronic wholesaler from China, our products are brand new and original. We are mainly sell all kinds of digital products, such as IPOD, laptop, LCD TV, camera, GPS, ps3, ▬▬▬ w w w 【 e b u y g g 】 c o m ▬▬▬ mobile phone, motorcycle and so on....... If you would like to order some of them, please contact us .
>
> # e b u y g g . com
> MSN : ebuygg ♦ @ ■ hotmail.com
> EMAIL : ebuygg ◇ @ ★ 188.com
> thank you for you reading ,hope for your reply in early best regards

Do you have a story that started on Hotmail? Tell us now

Fw: Big surprice ■▲◆⊕☉▲

Van: **HANS EELENS** (info@hanseelens.be)
Verzonden: donderdag 14 april 2011 21:45:35
Aan: s-p-a-m@live.com

----- Forwarded Message ----
From: red margar <redmargar@hotmail.com>
To: hans_asaert@yahoo.com
Sent: Sat, April 9, 2011 2:59:02 PM
Subject: Big surprice ■▲◆⊕○▲

Hello, friend,

Sorry to interrupt your precious time for a second. o

We are a big formal company who is specialized in selling digital and electrical products such as laptop,TV,digital camera, mobile, Digital Video, Mp4, GPS, and so on. l

All the items on our offical website are brand new in sealed factory boxes with offered warranty by original manufacturers. y

If you have free time, you can contact us:

□ (Our website: www . yahui-vip . com   Email: yahui_vip @ 188 . com)

4-9-2011

▲
⊕♀
◇☉●
△▲☉■
♀♀◆▲■
⊕▲♀♀♀△

BLESSED IS THE HAND THAT GIVETH

From: **Pieterjan Ginckels** (hello@pieterjanginckels.be)
Sent: Sat 1/22/11 8:56 PM
To: s-p-a-m@live.com

> From: "Mrs. Jennifer Wagner"<gvbilledo@eastwestbanker.com>
> Date: Sat 22 Jan 2011 18:39:35 CEST
> To: undisclosed-recipients:;
> Subject: BLESSED IS THE HAND THAT GIVETH
> Reply-To: < leonejones79@aol.com>
>
> Dear Friend.
>
> Good day and God bless you. I feel quite safe and satisfy dealing with you in this charity project.Though, this medium (Internet) has been greatly abused, I choose to reach you through it because it still remains the fastest, surest and most secured medium of communication. However, this correspondence is purely private, and it should be treated as such. As you read this, I don't want you to feel sorry for me, because, I believe everyone will die someday. My name is Mrs. Jennifer Wagner , a merchant in Dubai, in the U.A.E. I have been diagnosed with Esophageal cancer . It has defiled all forms of medical treatment, and right now I have only about a few months to live, according to medical experts.
>
> I have not particularly lived my life so well, As I never really cared for anyone(not even myself) but my business. Though I am very rich, I was never generous, I was always hostile to people and only focused on my business as that was the only thing I cared for. But now I regret all this as I now know that there is more to life than just wanting to have or make all the money in the world.
>
> I believe when God gives me a second chance to come to this world I would live my life a different way from how I have lived it. Now that God has called me, I have willed and given most of my property and assets to my immediate and extended family members as well as a few close friends.
>
> I want God to be merciful to me and accept my soul so, I have decided to give aims to charity organizations, as I want this to be one of the last good deeds I do on earth. So far, I have distributed money to some charity organizations in the U.A.E, Algeria and Malaysia. Now that my health has deteriorated so badly, I cannot do this myself anymore. I once asked members of my family to close one of my accounts and distribute the money which I have there to charity organization in Bulgaria and Pakistan, they refused and kept the money to themselves. Hence, I do not trust them anymore, as they seem not to be contended with what I have left for them.
>
> The last of my money which no one knows of is the huge cash deposit of TWELVE MILLION DOLLARS $12,000,000,that I have with a finance/Security Company abroad. I will want you to help me collect this deposit and dispatched it to charity organizations.
>
> I have set aside 25% for you and for your time if you want to help me to collect this Funds and also invest this money.
>
> N.B-PLEASE I WILL ADVISED YOU TO CONTACT THE ATTORNEY IN NETHERLANDS IMMEDIATELY, HE DOES EVERYTHING ON MY BEHALF AND HE'S VERY UNDERSTANDING AND I BELIEVE HE WILL LEAD YOU TO YOUR SUCCESS IN JESUS NAME AMEN.

Name: BARRISTER. LEONE EDWARD JONES

Email: leonejones79@aol.com

Remain blessed in the name of the Lord.

Yours in Christ,

Mrs. Jennifer Wagner

Find affordable Health Insurance - It's quick, Affordable and Easy

Van: **LowHealthInsuranceFromEclipseMediaOnline**
(LowHealthInsuranceFromEclipseMediaOnline@ig238.igarden4fun.com)
Verzonden: woensdag 19 januari 2011 8:18:06
Aan: ldb1062 (db1062@igarden4fun.com)

Find affordable Health Insurance - It's quick, Affordable and Easy

Breaking News: Refinance Rates at 2.99%! – See Details Now

Van: **LowMortgageRates** (LowMortgageRates@ig240.igarden4fun.com)
Verzonden: donderdag 20 januari 2011 1:30:35
Aan: ldb1004 (db1004@igarden4fun.com)

Breaking News: Refinance Rates at 2.99%! – See Details Now

FW: Letter for man.

From: **Steven** (steven@contourmechelen.be)
Sent: Tue 5/10/11 7:05 AM
To: s-p-a-m@live.com

Steven Op de Beeck
Contour Mechelen vzw
Sint-Romboutskerkhof 2
B - 2800 Mechelen
T +32 15 33 08 01
M +32 477 40 80 98
www.contour2011.be

-----Oorspronkelijk bericht-----
Van: iza@megafort.com.br [mailto:iza@megafort.com.br]
Verzonden: Geen
Aan: steven@contourmechelen.be
Onderwerp: Letter for man.

Hello my future friend!
I write to you the letter. And very much I hope to receive the answer from you.
Because it is very important for me. Also I hope that in the future my letter will make you happy.
My name is Marina. Me 30 years old. I was born in Russia. And now I live here.
I the beautiful woman. But still not met present love in Russia.
But now I would like to tell more about my letter to you.
The purpose in that that I shall soon have holiday from my work and I wish to visit the European country.
Also I shall receive my visa. And we could have a meeting.
Any country in the Western Europe. But my favorite Belgium.
I always dreamed to visit this fine country.
But I to not have friends or relatives in the Western Europe or in Belgium.
And consequently I have decided to write to you the letter.
For this purpose I have addressed in agency of acquaintances in my city. I live in city Cheboksary.
And this agency to give me yours e-mail.
Whether I do not know you are lonely. And whether to search you the woman for itself.
But I ask.............
I ask you to write to me the letter.
Because I very much would like to find the man which searches for love.
I think that it very romantically.
I when did not write the letter through the Internet earlier. But I of willows that so I can find the happiness.
Also I hope that you will write to me even 1 letter.
Also you can answer my questions.
- In what country you live now? In what city?
- You wish to meet the woman from Russia?
- Your heart is lonely now?

I hope that my letter will not complicate you and you to answer and send me
the photo.
I as shall send a photo to my following letter for you.
I think that you will love my photo.

Please, answer only my personal e-mail: mar1nazhandar@rambler.ru

The best regards,

Yours Marina.

Intimacy Killers!

From: **DoctorWilliams@Gmail.com**
Sent: Sat 12/25/10 7:00 AM
To: s-p-a-m@live.com

Here we go spamofficer...let's jump in and talk about the

Problems that contribute to a man's bedroom dysfunction

Just like David Letterman we have the Top Ten List for guys...

(10) Sexually transmitted diseases

These leave scarring, which obstructs the path of semen through the penis.

If the diseases occur in the testes, infertility results.

Your best protection: Always practice safe sex.

(9) Cardiovascular disease

Great sex for men depends on clear arteries. Most men know that being overweight increases their risk for heart disease but cardiovascular disease will destroy a man's sex life long before it kills him.

Reason?

When blood vessels are blocked, a man can't get the proper engorgement needed to achieve an erection.

Reversing atherosclerosis means better blood flow - and that translates to better erections and more sensitivity to touch. Those nerve endings that bring you so much pleasure during sex depend on good blood flow to be fully sensitized. Circulating blood disperses hormones, which regulate sexual function and response. And, of course, your heart has to be strong for the deep body, physical activity of lovemaking.

Avoid fatty fried foods and red meat. Eat more vegetables and salads.

(8) Lack of exercise

Exercise reduces tension, depression and anxiety. It increases self esteem,
positive attitude, the capacity for joy, mental acuity, aerobic capacity, energy, and libido. Even a brief aerobic workout can point your mood towards
lovemaking and encourage more intense orgasms.

Most men have no idea how closely regular exercise is linked to their sexual performance. During exercise, the body produces endorphins - the "feel-good" chemicals that increase arousal and orgasm intensity.

This sexy effect reportedly lasts 1 hour or more after just 10 minutes of activity.

In one new study, 78 healthy but sedentary men were studied during nine months of regular exercise.

The men exercised for 60 minutes a day, three days a week.

Every man in the study reported significantly enhanced sexuality, including increased frequency,
performance and satisfaction.

***Rising sexuality has even been correlated with the degree of fitness improvement!

The results were clear: The higher the level of physical fitness a man is able to attain,
the better his sex life***

(7) Drug reactions

Doctors rarely mention the many ways that drugs interfere with sex.

They worry (and rightly so) that men will be reluctant to take a drug that they know could
interfere with this basic human drive.

So, sexual side effects are hardly ever discussed when drugs are prescribed.

Besides lowering libido, drugs can cause drowsiness, lethargy, confusion, depression and weight gain.

Some drugs have a direct impact on brain chemistry.

Neurotransmitters, the brain's chemical messengers, are critical to sexual interest,
performance and enjoyment.

A wide range of medications - like antidepressants and high blood pressure medications - disrupt neurotransmitters, interfering with a man's ability to achieve erection or reach orgasm.

The result is extreme frustration - imagine the outcome if neither you or your partner know a drug is to blame?!

That's alot of info to digest for one day.

Make sure you forward these reports to your friends...including women!

Next report...you'll be SHOCKED with the findings.

Yours for better health,

Dr.R.Williams

To be removed, go to http://www.penisimprovement.com/cgi-bin/autoresponder/autoresponder.cgi?action=Remove&email=s-p-a-m@live.com

copyright penisimprovement.com

ĚŃ

ĚŇ

Creative entrepreneur in the dark

Art historians today may argue whether a work by Rembrandt can be ascribed to the master himself or to one of his students. For contemporary customers of the Baroque painter this was not the crucial question. It was more decisive that the painting was made in his style and was wearing his signature. So, in his studio in Leiden Rembrandt employed numerous assistants and students who copied his works or carried out his sketches according to his instructions. The results he sold as products of his own brand – a successful and profitable business model. In the 17th century, this worksharing process had nothing objectionable. Only a century later, in Romanticism, it became widely accepted that a work of art – ideally – had to be an output of the creative power of a singular genius. Lonesome attic instead of classroom or studio, originality rather than technical perfection was the credo.

Although the standards developed more than 200 years ago are persistently adopted until this day, when it comes to the question "Is this a piece of art or not?" Romanticism was just an episode. Since long, artists have returned to the former practice: "Whatever you do, don't do it yourself", as the German discursive pop band Tocotronic sings. This also sets out the motto for an up-to-date art production in a post-industrial society. Like in Rembrandt's time, artists don't have to prime their canvasses or produce a work themselves. Rather, today's artists are asked to develop ideas and initiate projects, delegate tasks or perform quality checks. Artists like Damien Hirst or Jeff Koons meet this personal profile perfectly, as does Olafur Eliasson. When the Danish-Icelandic artist creates an artificial waterfall in New York, he is supported by a many-headed project team, with himself as the leader. Eliasson accesses the knowhow of experts coming from very different fields – artists, physicists, engineers, technicians. His Berlin-based studio, which he runs like an entrepreneur, is his think tank, test laboratory and project office at the same time.

Pieterjan Ginckels, too, isn't particularly known for presenting himself as "the ingenious artist as creator". As Melanie Bono stated in her essay 'Pop Artz' (2008), Ginckels rather aims at "making his own diverse interests and ideas accessible as an experience for others". For example, in his project '1000 Beats' for the Neuer Aachener Kunstverein (NAK), Ginckels co-operated with a multitude of collaborators. He activated NAK members and friends, DJ Cristian Vogel and the Norwegian designer collective Grandpeople. Pieterjan Ginckels gave the impetus and offered a platform: People from the NAK network followed his appeal and provided record players, Vogel looped a one-second sample, which was pressed on vinyl and presented in a cover layout by Grandpeople. (Later, Pieterjan Ginckels appropriated this layout in a series of drawings). The track was continuously played from the record players arranged in a row in the NAK exhibition space.

S.P.A.M. OFFICE takes a collaborative approach, too. Through his website the artist requests e-mail addressees to forward spam e-mails to the office – as "raw material" for the artistic process. Pieterjan Ginckels is the project initiator and leader, while at the same time he appears as an entrepreneur and managing director. He recruits a team of employees, checks the minutely planned working process, criticizes the employees, motivates them, has an open ear for their concerns, controls whether the business plan has been fulfilled or not. Within an interior designed by himself, the staff has to provide a service for their director, who is their client as well. Their task is to screen the received e-mails, to sort useless e-mails out according to given formal criteria, to mark promising e-mails, paragraphs, phrases or single words on the printed e-mails, to classify and archive them. They act independently, they are free to make their own decisions, but the system in which they act is a strictly hierarchical one. In the entrance of the S.P.A.M. OFFICE in Be-Part in Waregem, a board shows an organogram of the company with the artist and patriarch on top. He is the ultimate decision maker in the firm: after an e-mail has passed all working stations in the office – from being examined and having the sender and interesting passages in the text marked to being archived in a file – the artist selects the e-mails, parts of the spam texts, or senders he considers suitable for his creative purposes.

S.P.A.M. OFFICE is a public agency; there is an "open house" whenever the staff is at work. The employees provide a "real" service, but their actions are also part of a performance taking place in the field of art. The artist is a "real" businessman, but at the same time he is not more than an artist posing as a businessman. True or staged, the final act, which S.P.A.M. OFFICE is targeted at, takes place outside opening hours and outside the office space: the creative transformation of archived materials into a haptic piece of art.

What the office work leads to, is visible for the employees as well as for the office visitors. The end result is placed on the wall of the "office building": lyrical, cryptic text cutouts, assembled into assumedly authentic dialogues or claims, or groups of modified and soundful terms. They are set in carefully selected fonts and layouts, which gives the series of characters an image-like quality, printed in A4 format or sometimes in poster or bill-board size, on glossy paper, attractively and suitably framed. All this is done according to criteria not presented to the public, only known by the artist. The creative act is the secret he holds; S.P.A.M. OFFICE is just a form of pre-production. Its performance ends in the archive – in Be-Part in an almost completely dark room – in ring binders silently lined up on dimly lit shelves. When and what the artist draws from out of these folders, which specific lines and words his eyes pick up and why they do so, how he modifies and varies the material, how he derives the final text and images from it, all that stays in the dark – in an even greater darkness than that of the archive room. The artist fulfils the creative act completely autonomously – here he is again: "the ingenious artist as creator"? Yes and no. Profoundly and playfully serious and with subtle irony, Pieterjan Ginckels demonstrates how disciplined, goal-oriented teamwork and an individual's creativity and originality can productively come together.

Jörg Kohnen-May, gallerist (von cirne Cologne), curator, communications expert

Å meaningful paycheck?

S.P.A.M. OFFICE covers a total of six workstations. The first workstation is the front office. Here, a first S.P.A.M. OFFICER prints out the incoming spam e-mails. When workload is low, this officer also undertakes activities that result in more incoming spam. The printed e-mails go to the back office where the pages are perforated and carefully bound with plastic rings. A third officer investigates the document and highlights the name of the sender with a fluorescent marker. Next, the paper is read in the spam lounge. Here it is decided whether or not the e-mail was handled properly. The e-mail is then ready to be archived. Archiving is the final act in the production chain that the spam runs through during the performance. A sixth officer is responsible for the facility management. His workstation is located at the office canteen, where coffee breaks, lunches, and work meetings take place.

It is not that the S.P.A.M. OFFICERS are pretending. At no time are volunteers asked to act. Participants are invited by the artist to participate in the work process in an authentic way. The artist himself plays the role of boss. He explains which jobs should be done at each workstation and shows the resources. Like the other officers, he wears the uniform with the company logo. His shirt, however, is white, unlike the cream of the performers. The artist controls the actions of the S.P.A.M. OFFICERS and is available for them to ask whether one is 'doing a good job'.

It is amazing to see how fast all participants feel comfortable with their roles as officers and get into the job. The different officers start to interact with each other, after the artist and 'manager' instructed them that they can go back if they think a mistake or inaccuracy has occurred. Automatically the officers use this interaction not only to rectify a single error, but also to improve the work process. This creates a system with unique feedback interaction, which resembles 'Total Quality Management' (TQM). Following the TQM principles, people who work within systems look for ways to continuously improve the system, and improve quality not only by detection, but by being preventative.

The interactions between the S.P.A.M. OFFICERS are interesting because they show that the S.P.A.M. OFFICERS are not simply acting but genuinely want to do their job well. The participants discuss different interpretations on whether the tasks were well performed. What at first seems a simple task, e.g. the identification of the sender, becomes a complex issue: is it the last-mentioned sender or rather the original sender of the e-mail? What do you do when there is only an e-mail address, or when names begin with a digit? During the performance, the officers really make an effort to deepen their tasks and in doing so, keep their work interesting. While the tasks at first glance seem banal for the participant as a spectator, they become very serious for the participant as a performer.

S.P.A.M. OFFICE is an obvious reference to 'scientific management', which considers a company as a closed system. In contrast, contemporary organizational theory assumes an organization as an open system in which social, economic and cultural factors play. In this sense, S.P.A.M. OFFICE is an anachronism. S.P.A.M. OFFICE also confronts us with some position practices. The ease with which the participants play their role can only be explained by a widespread familiarity – from their own experiences or through popular media – with this kind of mind-numbing office work. The talks between the participants, unknown to each other in advance, quickly center around clichés associated with familiar roles. This is particularly notable in their conversations about 'the boss', who rapidly is being called 'big chief'. Also, an officer who puts on a show for the boss becomes an object of ridicule and is called a 'boss pet'. Because of their joint position (subordinate of the boss) a certain 'esprit de corps' arises among the participants. The uniform also creates a certain identification with the S.P.A.M. OFFICE.

It is interesting to see how the structure of the office evolves through the different performances. At the start of the exhibition period, the e-mails were being classified based on the name of the sender. During the second performance day, the S.P.A.M. OFFICERS decided to use an additional thematic classification for the incoming e-mails. S.P.A.M. OFFICE is thus a dynamic exhibition. This is also apparent in the fact that 2D works of the artist ('S.P.A.M. dialogues') were added in the second retake of the exhibition. Combined with the office setting, they become an integral part of the performance and even affect it.

These graphical 'spam dialogues' based on textual elements in the archived spam e-mails inspire the officers as they show the ultimate goal of their labor. The 2D panels can indeed be considered as the 'end product' of the work. Like in most companies, employees can be motivated by the display of the final product. Work that is meaningless in itself – for example piercing holes in paper and putting plastic rings on the holes – becomes in that way meaningful. The need of modern (wo)man to do meaningful work is confirmed.
As labor became increasingly divided into subtasks (scientific management), and powerful administrations surrounding the production of goods and services emerged (bureaucratic way of working), the relationship between labor and objective became compromised. The meaning of work is no longer manifest and the need for meaningful work often remains unfulfilled. Therefore, in today's society meaning is being more and more achieved by limiting the 'horizon of meaning'. In other words, we prefer to be ignorant to the final consequences of our work. The meaning of work has shifted from the work itself (the product or service produced) to other aspects of employment such as wage (the paycheck at the end of the month), social contacts and social roles. We are not interested in what we do, but in how we work with each other, in the social identities that are constructed, and the relationships we maintain with each other. These aspects of work are important and meaningful. For those who are socially adapted to be part of labor organizations, a large part of their remuneration in the workplace is about having 'fun' with colleagues. These individuals develop activities and rituals that aim to ensure that even outsiders will consider their work important.

S.P.A.M. OFFICERS are in a similar position and lay bare these mechanisms. We do what we are supposed to do and we feel good about being part of an organization. We get respect from our colleagues. We have fun. This in itself makes the work meaningful. We are part of it. Because we do not want to lose this privilege, we do our job properly. We develop a certain work ethic and quality norm so that we do not lose our position. Others are thus excluded. In this fact, however, we are confronted with a permanent feeling of guilt.

The artist plays with this 'horizon of meaning'. First, he presents the 2D work as an end product of the S.P.A.M. OFFICE. Second, the ultimate significance or meaning of his art is very fragile. Here too, the aspect of fun is involved. It is not the social critique that drives the artist. S.P.A.M. OFFICERS are thus committed to the manager / artist without questioning his final product. They choose to limit their responsibility at this point and are waiting for the next paycheck.

Eva Platteau, Public Management Institute, KULeuven
Tine Holvoet, TeamTank, Brussels

A meaningful paycheck?

EN

Creative entrepreneur in the dark

Kunsthistorici van vandaag kunnen van mening verschillen over de vraag of een werk van Rembrandt kan toegeschreven worden aan de meester zelf of aan een van zijn leerlingen. Voor de toenmalige klanten van de barokschilder was dit niet de cruciale vraag. Meer doorslaggevend was dat het schilderij in zijn stijl was gemaakt en dat het zijn signatuur droeg. In zijn atelier in Leiden had Rembrandt dan ook vele assistenten en leerlingen in dienst, die zijn werken kopieerden of zijn schetsen uitvoerden volgens zijn instructies. De resultaten verkocht hij als producten van zijn eigen merk – een succesvol en winstgevend businessmodel.

In de 17de eeuw was er niets afkeurenswaardigs aan dit proces van werkverdeling. Pas een eeuw later, tijdens de romantiek, was men algemeen de mening toegedaan dat een kunstwerk – in het ideale geval – het resultaat moest zijn van de scheppende kracht van een individueel genie. Eenzaam zolderkamertje in plaats van leslokaal of atelier, originaliteit boven technische perfectie, dat was het credo. Hoewel de normen die meer dan tweehonderd jaar geleden werden ontwikkeld tot op vandaag nog steeds hardnekkig worden overgenomen, was de romantiek, als het gaat over de vraag 'Is dit een kunstwerk of niet?', slechts een fase. Kunstenaars zijn al lang teruggekeerd naar de vroegere praktijk: 'Wat je ook doet, doe het niet zelf', zoals de Duitse discursive-popgroep Tocotronic zingt. Dit geeft ook het motto aan voor een actuele kunstproductie in een postindustriële maatschappij. Net zoals in Rembrandts tijd hoeven kunstenaars niet zelf hun doeken te prepareren of een werk uit te voeren. Hedendaagse kunstenaars worden eerder gevraagd om ideeën te ontwikkelen en projecten in gang te zetten, taken te delegeren of kwaliteitscontroles uit te voeren. Kunstenaars zoals Damien Hirst of Jeff Koons voldoen perfect aan dit profiel, net als Olafur Eliasson. Wanneer deze Deens-IJslandse kunstenaar in New York een kunstmatige waterval creëert, wordt hij omringd door een veelkoppig projectteam, met hemzelf als teamleider. Eliasson doet een beroep op de knowhow van experts uit heel uiteenlopende gebieden – kunstenaars, fysici, ingenieurs, technici. Zijn Berlijnse studio, die hij runt als een ondernemer, is tegelijkertijd zijn denktank, testlaboratorium en projectbureau.

Ook Pieterjan Ginckels staat er niet meteen voor bekend dat hij zich voordoet als 'de ingenieuze kunstenaar als schepper'. Zoals Melanie Bono schreef in haar essay 'Pop Artz' (2008), wil Ginckels eerder 'zijn eigen diverse interesses en ideeën toegankelijk maken als een ervaring voor anderen'. In zijn project '1000 Beats' voor de Neuer Aachener Kunstverein (NAK), bijvoorbeeld, werkte Ginckels samen met een heleboel partners. Hij mobiliseerde NAK-leden en vrienden, dj Cristian Vogel en het Noorse vormgeverscollectief Grandpeople. Pieterjan Ginckels gaf de aanzet en bood een platform aan: mensen van het NAK-netwerk gaven gehoor aan zijn oproep en bezorgden platenspelers, Vogel maakte een loop van een sample van 1 seconde, die in vinyl werd geperst en gepresenteerd werd in een coverontwerp van Grandpeople. (Pieterjan Ginckels eigende zich die vormgeving later toe in een reeks tekeningen.) De track werd doorlopend gespeeld op de platenspelers die in een rij waren opgesteld in de tentoonstellingsruimte van het NAK.

Ook S.P.A.M. OFFICE gaat uit van een gezamenlijke benadering. Via zijn website verzoekt de kunstenaar ontvangers van e-mails om spam-e-mails naar het kantoor te forwarden – als 'basismateriaal' voor het artistieke proces. Pieterjan Ginckels is de initiatiefnemer en de leider van het project, terwijl hij terzelfdertijd optreedt als een ondernemer en als managing director. Hij recruteert een team van bedienden, controleert het minutieus geplande werkproces, geeft kritiek op de werknemers, motiveert hen, heeft een luisterend oor voor hun bekommernissen en controleert of het businessplan wordt nagekomen of niet. In een interieur dat hij zelf heeft ontworpen moeten de personeelsleden een dienst leveren aan hun directeur, die ook hun klant is. Het is hun taak de ontvangen e-mails te screenen, onbruikbare e-mails eruit te sorteren volgens welbepaalde formele criteria, veelbelovende e-mails, paragrafen, zinnen of afzonderlijke woorden op de uitgeprinte e-mails te markeren, ze te ordenen en te archiveren. Ze werken zelfstandig, ze hebben de vrijheid om hun eigen beslissingen te nemen, maar het systeem waarin ze werken is strikt hiërarchisch. Aan de ingang van S.P.A.M. OFFICE in Be-Part in Waregem hangt een bord met daarop een organogram van het bedrijf, met bovenaan de kunstenaar en stichter. Hij is de ultieme decisionmaker in de firma: nadat een e-mail alle werkstations in het kantoor is gepasseerd – van het onderzoeken over het markeren van de afzender en interessante passages in de tekst tot het archiveren in een map – selecteert de kunstenaar die e-mails, stukken van de spamteksten of afzenders die hij bruikbaar acht voor zijn creatief plan.

S.P.A.M. OFFICE is een openbare instelling; er is een 'open huis' telkens wanneer het personeel aan het werk is. De bedienden leveren een 'echte' dienst, maar hun handelingen maken ook deel uit van een performance die plaatsvindt op het gebied van kunst. De kunstenaar is een 'echte' zakenman, maar tegelijkertijd is hij niet meer dan een kunstenaar die zich voordoet als een zakenman. Echt of in scène gezet, de uiteindelijke handeling, waarop S.P.A.M. OFFICE gericht is, vindt plaats buiten de openingsuren en buiten de kantoorruimte: de creatieve transformatie van archiefmateriaal tot een haptisch kunstwerk.

Waar het bureauwerk toe leidt, is zichtbaar voor zowel de werknemers als de bezoekers van het kantoor. Het eindresultaat wordt aan de muur van het 'kantoorgebouw' bevestigd: lyrische, cryptische tekstknipsels, geassembleerd tot vermeend authentieke dialogen of stellingen, of groepen van gewijzigde en melodieuze termen. Ze zijn gezet in zorgvuldig geselecteerde fonts en dito lay-out, waardoor de reeks karakters er gaat uitzien als een afbeelding, geprint op A4-formaat of soms op poster- of billboardformaat, op glanzend papier, aantrekkelijk en passend ingelijst. Dit alles is uitgevoerd volgens criteria die niet aan het publiek worden meegedeeld, maar enkel door de kunstenaar gekend zijn. De creatieve handeling is het geheim dat hij bewaart; S.P.A.M. OFFICE is slechts een vorm van preproductie. De uitvoering ervan eindigt in het archief – in Be-Part in een bijna volledig donkere ruimte – in ringmappen die zwijgend in het gelid staan op zwak belichte rekken. Wanneer en wat de kunstenaar uit deze mappen haalt, op welke specifieke regels en woorden zijn oog valt en waarom, hoe hij het materiaal aanpast en afwisselt, hoe hij de uiteindelijke teksten en beelden eraan ontleent, dat alles blijft in het duister – in een duisternis die zelfs nog dieper is dan die van de archiefruimte. De kunstenaar volbrengt de creatieve handeling volledig autonoom – daar is hij weer: 'de ingenieuze kunstenaar als schepper'? Ja en neen. Diepgaand en speels ernstig en met subtiele ironie toont Pieterjan Ginckels aan hoe gedisciplineerd, doelgericht teamwerk en de creativiteit en originaliteit van een individu productief kunnen samenkomen.

Jörg Kohnen-May, galerist (von cirne Keulen), curator, communicatie-expert

Å meaningful paycheck?

S.P.A.M. OFFICE omvat in totaal zes werkposten. Een eerste werkpost is het frontoffice, waar een eerste S.P.A.M. OFFICER de inkomende spam-e-mails uitprint. Op minder drukke momenten onderneemt deze *officer* zelf activiteiten die ertoe leiden dat meer spam het e-mailadres bereikt. De uitgeprinte mail wordt in het backoffice geperforeerd en de gaatjes worden voorzien van plastic ringetjes. Een derde *officer* onderzoekt de spammail en duidt de afzender aan met fluostift. Gelezen wordt het document in de *spam lounge*. Hier wordt beslist of de mail correct behandeld werd en gearchiveerd mag worden. In het archief sorteert een vijfde *officer* alle documenten in mappen. Hier eindigt de productieketen die de spam-e-mail doormaakt tijdens de performance. Een zesde *officer* is verantwoordelijk voor het *facility management* in de aan het archief grenzende kantoorkantine. Hier vinden de koffiepauzes, lunches en werkvergaderingen plaats.

Het is niet zo dat de S.P.A.M. OFFICERS moeten 'doen alsof'. Op geen enkel moment wordt hen gevraagd te acteren. De deelnemers worden door de kunstenaar uitgenodigd om op een authentieke wijze aan het arbeidsproces deel te nemen. Zelf vervult hij de rol van baas. Hij legt uit welke taken aan welke werkpost moeten worden uitgevoerd en welke hulpmiddelen er ter beschikking zijn. Net als de andere *officers* draagt hij het uniform met het logo van de firma, alleen is zijn hemd wit en niet crèmekleurig zoals dat van de performers. Hij controleert de goede uitvoering van de taken en is beschikbaar voor de *officers*, die aan hem kunnen vragen 'of ze wel goed bezig zijn'.

Het is verbazingwekkend te zien hoe snel iedereen in zijn rol kruipt en aan de slag gaat. Interactiemomenten tussen de deelnemers ontstaan snel, doordat de kunstenaar en baas de instructie geeft dat elke S.P.A.M. OFFICER kan teruggaan naar een vorige fase in de keten wanneer hij of zij van oordeel is dat er een fout of onnauwkeurigheid is gebeurd. Automatisch hanteren de *officers* deze interactie, niet alleen om een fout eenmalig recht te zetten maar ook om het proces te verbeteren, om elkaar als het ware bij te sturen. Zo ontstaat er een systeem met verschillende feedbackmomenten of terugkoppelingen, dat doet denken aan 'Total Quality Management' (TQM). Hierbij streven de mensen die binnen het systeem werken naar continue verbetering en zorgen ze via preventie en detectie van fouten voor kwaliteit.

De interactiemomenten tussen de S.P.A.M. OFFICERS zijn interessant, omdat ze duidelijk maken dat de *officers* niet acteren, maar gewoon hun job goed willen doen. Verschillende interpretaties over 'wanneer een taak goed is uitgevoerd' worden bijvoorbeeld met elkaar geconfronteerd. Wat op het eerste gezicht een eenvoudige taak lijkt, zoals de naam van de afzender van de e-mail identificeren en aanduiden, blijkt vaak een complex gegeven te zijn: wordt de laatste afzender aangeduid of eerder de originele spamverzender? Wat doe je wanneer enkel het mailadres te lezen valt, en wat met namen die met een cijfer beginnen? De S.P.A.M. OFFICERS doen moeite om zich in hun taak te verdiepen en proberen hierdoor hun taak boeiend te houden. Hoe stompzinnig deze taak voor de deelnemer als toeschouwer ook lijkt, zo serieus wordt ze voor de deelnemer als performer.

S.P.A.M. OFFICE is een duidelijke verwijzing naar de wetenschappelijke bedrijfsvoering (*scientific management*), die een bedrijf als een gesloten systeem beschouwt. In de hedendaagse organisatieleer wordt er daarentegen van uitgegaan dat een organisatie een open systeem is, waar sociale, economische en culturele factoren op inspelen. In die zin is S.P.A.M. OFFICE een anachronisme. Anderzijds confronteert S.P.A.M. OFFICE ons met bepaalde *position practices*. Het gemak waarmee de deelnemers in hun rol kruipen, kan enkel verklaard worden door een wijdverspreid vertrouwd zijn – uit directe ervaring ofwel via populaire media – met dit soort afstompend kantoorwerk. De gesprekken tussen de deelnemers, die elkaar nog niet op voorhand kennen, gaan al snel over de clichés die verbonden zijn met vertrouwde rollenpatronen. Opvallend is ook het samenspannen tegen 'de baas'. De baas krijgt bijvoorbeeld de bijnaam *'big chief'*. Of iemand die te hard zijn best doet, wordt streber of 'bazenpoeper' genoemd. Doorheen hun gezamenlijke positie (ondergeschikt aan de baas) ontstaat een bepaalde *esprit de corps* tussen de deelnemers. Het uniform creëert ook een bepaalde identificatie als medewerker van S.P.A.M. OFFICE.

Interessant om te zien is hoe de structuur van het kantoor evolueert doorheen de verschillende performances. Bij aanvang van de tentoonstellingsperiode werden de mails enkel op naam gearchiveerd. Tijdens de tweede performancedag beslisten de S.P.A.M. OFFICERS om een bijkomende thematische classificatie in te voeren. S.P.A.M. OFFICE is ook in elke reproductie in beweging: de 2D-S.P.A.M.-dialogen werden pas op de tweede tentoonstellingsplek gecombineerd met de kantoorsetting en beïnvloeden de performance. Of beter, ze maken integraal deel uit van S.P.A.M. OFFICE. Deze grafische 'spamdialogen' van de kunstenaar, gebaseerd op tekstuele elementen van de gearchiveerde spammails, inspireren de S.P.A.M. OFFICERS omdat ze tonen wat het einddoel van hun arbeid is. De 2D-panelen kunnen immers beschouwd worden als het finale eindproduct van het werkproces. Zoals in klassieke bedrijven worden de medewerkers gemotiveerd door de voorspiegeling van het eindproduct. Werk dat op zich betekenisloos is – gaatjes met de perforator prikken en plastic ringetjes op de gaatjes plakken – krijgt zo toch betekenis. De behoefte van de hedendaagse mens om zinvol werk te doen wordt bevestigd.

Doordat het arbeidsproces enerzijds opgesplitst raakte in deeltaken (*scientific management*), en doordat er anderzijds machtige administraties zijn ontstaan rond het produceren van goederen en diensten (bureaucratische manier van werken) is de band tussen arbeid en product gecompromitteerd. Hierdoor is het niet steeds duidelijk wat de zin van het werk nog is en blijft de behoefte naar zinvol werk vaak onvervuld. In een kapitalistische samenleving wordt zingeving daarom meer en meer bereikt door het inperken van de 'horizon van betekenis'. We stellen ons met andere woorden liever geen vragen over waar ons werk finaal toe dient. De zin van het werk wordt verschoven van het werk zelf (het product of de dienst die gemaakt wordt) naar andere aspecten van het werk zoals het loon (de *paycheck* op het einde van de maand), de sociale contacten en de sociale rollen die erbij horen. Wat we doen, boet aan belang in, maar hoe we op het werk met elkaar omgaan, de sociale identiteiten die geconstrueerd worden, de relaties die we met elkaar onderhouden, zijn belangrijk en betekenisvol. Voor de mensen die sociaal aangepast zijn aan deze situatie is een groot deel van hun beloning op het werk de 'fun' die ze kunnen maken met collega's. Deze zogenaamde *haves* ontwikkelen activiteiten en rituelen die als doel hebben ervoor te zorgen dat hun werk belangrijk wordt geacht door buitenstaanders. De S.P.A.M. OFFICERS bevinden zich in een gelijkaardige positie en leggen dit mechanisme bloot. We doen wat ons gevraagd wordt omdat we ons goed voelen als we deel uitmaken van een organisatie. We krijgen aanzien en respect van onze collega's. We hebben 'fun'. Dit maakt het werk op zich zinvol. We horen erbij. Omdat we dit voorrecht niet willen verliezen, doen we ons werk goed. We ontwikkelen een bepaald arbeidsethos en kwaliteitsnormen, zodat we onze positie niet verliezen. Anderen worden zo uitgesloten. Dit gegeven confronteert ons echter met een permanent schuldgevoel. De kunstenaar speelt met deze zingevingshorizon. Enerzijds presenteert hij het 2D-werk als een eindproduct van S.P.A.M. OFFICE. Anderzijds is de ultieme betekenis of zingeving van zijn eigen kunst heel broos. Ook hier speelt het aspect van 'fun' een rol. Het is immers niet de maatschappijkritiek die de kunstenaar drijft. De S.P.A.M. OFFICERS zetten zich in voor de baas / kunstenaar zonder zijn eindproduct in vraag te stellen. Ze kiezen ervoor daar hun verantwoordelijkheid te laten ophouden. En te wachten op de volgende *paycheck*.

Eva Platteau, Instituut voor de Overheid, KULeuven
Tine Holvoet, TeamTank, Brussel

APE#011
Gent, Belgium
info@artpapereditions.org
www.artpapereditions.org

ISBN 9789490800031
© 2011, Art Paper Editions and
Pieterjan Ginckels

S.P.A.M. BOOK
Concept: Pieterjan Ginckels
Coordination: Patrick Ronse
Graphic design: Jurgen Maelfeyt
Photographs: Olmo Peeters and Pieterjan Ginckels
Texts: Jörg Kohnen-May, Eva Platteau,
Tine Holvoet
Text editing and translation: Mia Verstraete
Printing: Cassochrome Waregem

The release of this book coincides with the exhibition 'S.P.A.M. OFFICE' of Pieterjan Ginckels organized by Be-Part Center for Contemporary Art, Waregem, Belgium, (May 7th till May 15th 2011), and has been published with the support of the Executive of the Provincial Council of West Flanders, consisting of Mr Paul Breyne, Governor-chairman, Mr Dirk De fauw, Mr Patrick Van Gheluwe, Mrs Marleen Titeca-Decraene, Mr Gunter Pertry, Mr Bart Naeyaert and Mr Guido Decorte, Members, and Mr Hilaire Ost, Provincial Clerk.

Be-Part, Center for Contemporary Art
Coordination / Artistic director: Patrick Ronse
Communication: Provincie West-Vlaanderen:
Communication Department; Pieter Vansteenbrugge
Exhibition assistants: Frank Temmerman, Marc Vermeersch, Marjan Nolf
Additional exhibition building: Aorta+
Workshops: kleinVerhaal: Dieter Debruyne, Anne De Loof
Westerlaan 17, B-8790 Waregem (Belgium)
T + 32 56 62 94 10 – www.be-part.be

Works in the exhibition courtesy Galerie de Expeditie, Zsa-Zsa Eyck
Amsterdam, Netherlands
galerie@de-expeditie.com
www.de-expeditie.com

Many thanks to the S.P.A.M. OFFICERS: Hilde Baert, Patrice Bevernage, Rita Bonny, Thomas Dekeyser, Benoît Dendooven, Yvan Derwéduwé, Annelies Feys, Martijn Gillaerts, Tine Holvoet, Catherine Molleman, Eva Platteau, Sven Poupaert, Daphne Ronse, Patrick Ronse, Sandrine Rosseel, Rony Smessaert, Jeroen Van Assche, Sofie Vandenbroeck, Christof Vanderghinste, Pieter Vansteenbrugge, Marc Vermeersch, Veronique Viane, Joan Weehaeghe.

Thanks to Provincie West-Vlaanderen, Department Comm@: Ann Tavernier; Department HRM: Hilde Vandromme; werkgroep Be-Part. Special thanks to Galerie de Expeditie Amsterdam: Zsa-Zsa Eyck; Frauke Dendooven.

Pieterjan Ginckels thanks TeamTank; Be-Part; Zsa-Zsa Eyck; the authors; S.P.A.M. OFFICERS; spam mail senders; friends, family, fans.

To ---***Roderick 1dayFly***---

Printed in Belgium
First print: june 2011

With the support of

Be-Part is a member of **PARTIZAN** hedendaagse kunst in West-Vlaanderen